KISS
I'm not good enough
GOODBYE

a 3-step system for destroying your fears and boosting your self-confidence

Marie Eve Plamondon

Copyright © 2016 Marie Eve Plamondon

All rights reserved.

ISBN: 978-1530934447
ISBN-13: 1530934443

DEDICATION

To my wonderful man, Guillaume, the eternal dreamer! None of my goals are too crazy for him. He's my shield; he protects my positive thinking against negative vibes.

I love you *chéri*

WHAT WE'LL TALK ABOUT IN THIS BOOK

1	Register this book and get free updates and resources	1
2	How to use this book	2
3	Hello! Nice to meet you.	5
4	Lesson 1: Confidence is a skill	14
5	Lesson 2: Confidence can change your life	20
6	Lesson 3: How to become a fear destroyer	26

REGISTER THIS BOOK
AND GET FREE UPDATES AND RESOURCES

If you'd like to receive free updates of this book and awesome useful resources, visit
https://marieeveplamondon.com/bookbonus
or send me an email at marie@marieeveplamondon.com.

MARIE EVE PLAMONDON

HOW TO USE THIS BOOK

**You've got great potential.
But your lack of confidence holds you back.**

When it comes to self-confidence, you're:
- tired of living an unfulfilled and unhappy life
- stuck in old patterns
- feeling you could achieve so much more in life

Good news: I can definitely help you with that.
Confidence is a skill, so it can be trained.

This book is for...
Serious people, people who are tired of living an unfulfilled and unhappy life, people who could achieve so much more in life, people who are stuck and are looking for a way out.

This book is NOT for...
Lazy people who are NOT willing to put in the work to

improve their life, people who are looking for a magic potion or magic pill, people who are NOT committed and NOT willing to change.

You can use this book however you want. However (Oh! two *howevers* in two sentences, with two different meanings, score!), here's what I suggest.

The book is divided in 3 main parts and each one represents a lesson (I've been a teacher so lessons make sense to me and hopefully they'll make sense to you too). Each lesson presents a specific topic, examples, and challenges. The challenges are like your homework, your assignments, what you should do to implement what you've learned in the lesson. Make sure you're taking your challenges seriously. They are the key to your transformation: from insecure (or not so confident) to confident. They are your confidence boosters!

And go back to this book every time you feel that your self-confidence or your fears are controlling your life.

This book is by no means a quick fix. I have to say that I don't believe in quick fixes of any kind. I truly believe that great things come to people who put the work into it. Karma. Karma can be a bitch. It can also be your BFF, if you're respectful and a kind person.

So you won't resolve all your self-confidence issues just by reading this book. Think of self-confidence as food for your happiness, just like vegetables are food for your body. You have to eat every single day, for the rest of your life to be healthy and have energy, and be alive!

It's the same for your self-confidence. You'll need to use the tips I provide in this book every single day, for the rest of your life.

Don't forget to register your book to get access to your bonuses: https://marieeveplamondon.com/bookbonus or send me an email at marie@marieeveplamondon.com.

Throughout the book, I'll suggest actions you can take to go further in boosting your self-confidence. You'll have a great start with what you'll learn in this book, but that's only the first step. With my programs, you'll go deeper and so create a greater transformation. From insecure to confident!

I love to hear your stories, questions and comments so please do not hesitate to contact me.

Facebook
www.facebook.com/marieeveplamondoninc

Twitter
www.twitter.com/marie_eve_plam

Pinterest
www.pinterest.com/marieeveplam/

Website
https://marieeveplamondon.com

KISS *I'm not good enough* GOODBYE

HELLO! NICE TO MEET YOU.

My name is Marie and I'm your self-confidence booster.

Before I tell you my story I want to make something clear.

> My parents love and have loved me with all their heart. I know that. And I also love them very much.
>
> However their insecurities (fears) push them to try to stop me whenever I have creative ideas. They're also very comfortable sharing their opinion with me, no matter how emotionally painful it can be. They don't do it on purpose, but let's just say that I had to work hard to overcome their judgment and grow my self-confidence

There has always been a part of me that wanted to help others, but I could never pinpoint how I could achieve my goal. I didn't want to be a doctor, but I could feel other people's pain. I didn't want to be a psychologist, but I could help my friends get through tough times. I didn't want to be a teacher, but... wait. Oh yes! I've been a teacher.

If you'd asked me what I wanted to be when I grew up, I would never in a million years have said a self-confidence booster. Never. Why not? Well I wasn't born in a confidence bath, far from it.

I was raised in a lower middle-class family in Quebec, Canada. My mom has worked in a grocery store for over 30 years and my dad has just retired as a plant handyman – not that it was his official title, but he tried almost all job assignments available over the years.

During my teenage years, I was quite lucky because I was considered pretty. I had friends and wasn't really intimidated. However, I never felt like I could do great things: I received good grades, but I had to study like crazy. I *had to* because I could never remember what was said during class once the class was over. I'm very good at memorizing things – but not at understanding them...

My parents were happy with my report cards, as long as I had grades higher than average. Sometimes, they would ask me why I didn't get higher grades. I would say that I got higher than the average, but it didn't seem to be enough anymore. That's when I started to feel their disappointment and realized that I wasn't doing enough to earn their praise.

As I grew older, I wasn't sure what to do with my life. So I followed what society told me to do. I finished high school, and went to CEGEP – one of the many special Quebec things that make us different. I successfully completed a technical program in fashion merchandising. I tried to dropout of the program several times but my parents told me to finish what I'd started.

During that program, my father told me something that I'll never forget. (Remember that we love each other very much.) He said that no matter how hard I would try, I would end up being a cashier at Wal-Mart... That hurt. A lot. (I don't want to sound arrogant by saying that, but a technical degree prepares you for a profession and so that's what I felt like I deserved at that point in my life.) I gave him the silent treatment and, after 2 days, it was like it never happened.

Then I went to university to study communications. My parents were *so* proud of me for getting a higher education. They didn't get a chance to get one; in fact, they didn't complete high school. My dad had to start bringing money home for his family. My mom's parents believed that it wasn't worth it to send a woman to university... Times have changed, thankfully.

When I finally completed my bachelor, I was so ecstatic. I got a job right away and I was learning from amazing people. After 2 years, I got bored, so I changed jobs and went to work for another employer. Same excitement at first and then, boredom. I did that with my first 3 employers.

The same thing was happening in my love life. Fireworks and then, nothing. You might think that it was because I was still young. Maybe that's true. In that case, why did it suddenly change? I wouldn't say overnight, but over the course of less than a year.

I'll tell you. I met someone who's a dreamer, who's not afraid to push the limits, who reacts to my crazy dreams by saying, "Cool! Go for it. Is there anything I can do to help?"

What? No condescending comments? No "You can always dream"? No "when will you finally settle down"? None of that. Only kind and encouraging words.

That person is my life partner, Guillaume. ☺

After I met my dreamer, I changed jobs one more time, and finally decided to try something completely new, a real challenge: proofreading as a freelancer – so self-employed.

I did it because I had his support. Not that I needed *his* support, but I needed some kind of support and I knew I couldn't get it from the people around me.

My parents were quite disappointed by my decision, as you might imagine. They said I should settle down, that no job is perfect so why change again, I had good benefits, and so forth. Their lack of support hurt, again.

After being self-employed for almost 2 years, I decided to change careers (Again, I know!) and move to another province. Well not just another province, but another coast: from the East to the West coast, from proofreading to teaching.

I wanted to do something that would mean something, to feel that I was contributing to the better good.

When I first thought about going back to university to change careers, Guillaume's reaction was "That's a good idea! What do you have to do to get your certification?" He was *still* supporting my decision 100%. Wow! ☺

What was my parents' reaction? You guessed it: disappointment, again, and frustration. And they can be quite verbal with their opinion. Fights, silent treatments, and condescending statements were somewhat expected, but still very hurtful.

They told me that I was lost, that I wasn't doing what I was supposed to (buy a house, have children, get married), that I was regressing, and basically that it was a terrible idea.

What was a girl in my position supposed to do? The old me would have argued with them. The new me decided that it wasn't worth it. My mind was made up and I was happy with my decision. (My self-confidence was starting to grow!)

So I got certified as a teacher. As a student-teacher, I had to write my credo, my teaching philosophy if you will. It was pretty clear to me: I wanted to help teenagers be more confident. That was it! Pretty simple you might say, but oh-so-challenging on a day-to-day basis.

Yes, I did manage to find ways to grow some students' self-esteem, but it wasn't enough for my liking. The time-consuming elements of a teacher's job got in the way of my mission: the report cards, the assignments, the homework, the lack of time to connect on a meaningful basis with students, just to name a few.

I thought to myself "there has to be a better way". With my credo in mind, I started my very own business, which turned out to be the best decision I've made so far in my life.

When I met Guillaume, I wanted to figure out what was wrong with me, why I wasn't able to stay motivated at my job, why I was never really happy with what I had.

Yes, Guillaume changed my world. Even though he represents the first step towards my self-confidence healing, I wouldn't be where I am today if I'd stopped there. I had to continue on this path full of possibilities and dreams. But I was so not used to that! I got lost several times and had to find a way to get back on the right track every time.

What I mean is that you may need a little push from someone to finally take action, and that's ok! However, your transformation from insecure to confident cannot happen without you. You're the essential ingredient.

I know some people who went through an addiction rehab and one of the things they learned is how vital YOU are in the equation. It's the same when you want to change something about yourself, about your thinking, your mindset. You can read as many books, meet as many life coaches as you want; in the end YOU are your own solution.

Like I said, I wanted to know what was wrong with me. After intensive research and introspection, I noticed that 2 elements were stopping me from reaching my goals and my full potential: self-confidence (or lack thereof) and fear (I should say fears).

Everything we do (and don't do) is linked to self-confidence and fears. One of the things I figured out is that I was the main reason my self-confidence was so fragile. But there's an upside: I was also the person who could boost my self-confidence. It was such a relief… and stressful at the same time. I had so much work to do.

The hardest part was to rewire my brain completely. It was so challenging. But I'm really thankful I did, because I'm now my true self: no excuses, no mask, me. And I'm now proud of myself, for my transformation and for giving back to others.

My quest wasn't straightforward. It took me a lot of perseverance to do it all by myself, but I did it. And now I can share my story and my knowledge with you, to help you get what you want and what you deserve in life.

I've always worked to help people boost their self-confidence: I've helped spokespersons, people with depression, teenagers, and grown-ups. But most importantly, I helped myself. And I encourage you to do the same, for your sake and the sake of people around you.

Tell me: marie@marieeveplamondon.com

In your life, what are the obstacles to achieve your goals and dreams? Relatives? Guilt? Fear? Friends? Pessimists? Society?

If you'd like to learn how to get over your obstacles, make sure to join the Self-Confidence Boosters' family.

Facebook: Self-Confidence Boosters group

Website: https://marieeveplamondon.com

Want to know more about me? Add me on Facebook and Twitter. I'd love to e-meet you. ;)

Facebook
www.facebook.com/marieeveplamondoninc

Twitter
www.twitter.com/marie_eve_plam

Ok enough about me. Let's start your transformation!

LESSON 1
CONFIDENCE IS A SKILL

No one is born with confidence, because confidence is a skill, which means it can be trained. That's great news because *you* control it; *you* have the power to boost it. You're in charge!

In this lesson, I'll explain why I see confidence as a skill. At the end, just like I do in all my programs, I'll give you small challenges to put what you've learned today into practice.

Ok let's get started, shall we?

WHAT'S A SKILL?
A skill is an ability that you've learned. And that's the important part: that you've learned. So you're not born with your skills. You learn them.

And how do we learn new things? Practice, practice, practice. And you need to be careful: if you don't practice your skill regularly, it will decrease.

Have you ever stopped doing something you were good at and decided one day to go back to it? Were you surprised by how much your skill had gone downhill? Of course it went downhill! Like I said, a skill is something that you learn. So you need repetition, repetition, repetition to keep it.

Let's say you want to learn a second or third language, like French. You practice intensively for 2 months by spending your whole summer in France. You come back home and stop practicing French. Summer arrives and you go to France again. Do you think your French will be as good as when you left France, at the end of last summer? Of course not! You didn't take care of your skill; you didn't practice. Do you see my point?

It's the same with confidence. You need momentum. You need to practice your confidence skill every single day, for the rest of your life. Yep!

WHAT'S CONFIDENCE?
Confidence means trusting someone or something. Here we're talking about self-confidence, having confidence in yourself, trusting your abilities, qualities, and judgment.

In short, it's a feeling that you're _____ enough. People who aren't confident doubt themselves.

In my opinion, self-confidence is the most important skill ever. I know, I'm bias, but self-confidence is what allows you to reach your full potential. And that's my goal. I want *you* to reach your full potential.

MY STORY
Now I'll share with you a story to make sense of all of this.

Maybe you know a little bit about me, maybe you don't. But here's my story.

Growing up, my life was quite ordinary. I didn't wish to change the world. I didn't have big dreams, big goals.

Maybe it's because I didn't believe in myself. Maybe it's because my parents didn't have great expectations for me. Whatever the reason, I was living a passive life with nothing extraordinary.

Then it hit me. I was never truly happy and I didn't have a clear sense of purpose. I felt like I wasn't complete, I was unfulfilled. I thought my life could be so much better, you know?

So I decided to make a list of everything I wanted in life. In fact, I started with a list I'd made when I was a teenager. Some goals weren't relevant anymore (to own a pink cellphone for example), but some goals were still very relevant, to my surprise.

Then it was time to figure out why I hadn't attained those goals yet. I made another list, a list of roadblocks. It took me several weeks to complete it. My conclusion was that fear and low self-confidence were controlling my life, and my happiness.

So began my quest to learn everything about fear and self-confidence. Well maybe not everything, but it was the only thing on my mind.

One thing I figured out during my research was that I'm the main reason my self-confidence was so fragile: me. But there's an upside to that: I'm also the person who can boost my self-confidence. So I did a little experiment to see if this conclusion was correct. And it was because it worked!

What I've learned during my research really changed my life. Trust me! I had to rewire my brain completely and it was challenging. I had to change the way I speak, think, everything. I was constantly analyzing myself to improve. At first it was exhausting. But bit-by-bit, it became easier. Now it's like second nature to me!

But don't get me wrong: my formula is not magical. I still need to work on my self-confidence every single day and you'll need to do the same. It's a life-long training. But it's also the best training to reach your full potential.

You want an example of a situation where I still need to work on my self-confidence? Well... every time I record a video or speak English.

I chose to offer my services in English, even though I was born and raised in Quebec; you know the province of Canada, on the East Coast, where people speak *only* French? Yes, that one.

Long story short: I have an accent when I speak English. It bothers me, but I keep on talking anyway. That's when I control my self-confidence. When my self-confidence controls me, I shut up, I'm afraid to say something stupid because expressing my thoughts in English is harder than in French.

When I say that, some people ask me why I don't just offer my services in French, it would be easier, right?

But I don't want to, for 2 reasons:

1. I like that it's a challenge, it means it's important. I know that each time I'm doing something challenging, it's an opportunity to grow, to improve.

2. I want to reach as many people as possible with my services. I want to help others by sharing what I've learned during my quest, especially because I've seen such great results.

CHALLENGES

Ok enough about me. Time for your challenges. Woop woop!

So your challenges for today's lesson are:

1. Make a list of your goals.
2. Make a list of your roadblocks.

BONUS: Send me an email to share your story and receive free tips and tricks: marie@marieeveplamondon.com

LESSON 2
CONFIDENCE CAN CHANGE YOUR LIFE

People who are confident feed their brains with positive thoughts. We can say that thinking is the reflection of your self-confidence. But it's more than that because thinking regulates action. So if you want to improve your action and your thinking, you have to work on your self-confidence.

In this lesson, I'll explain how confidence can change your life. Let's just say for now that confidence affects every aspect of your life. (And if you're in business, you need to pay even more attention to it because it's related to your credibility.)

CONFIDENCE AND CHALLENGES
Life is full of unexpected experiences, some challenging, some really exciting. Whether you see that statement as

being positive or negative depends on your level of self-confidence.

As I said in the previous lesson, challenges are opportunities to grow and get better at something.

No matter the challenge or the opportunity, you should remember that you're in your prime today. Don't be too nostalgic by saying: oh if I'd known this when I was 20, I would have been able to do it, but today, I'm too old.

That's negative thinking because you're looking for excuses. Be realistic instead. Let me tell you a little secret: You're the youngest you'll ever be. So now's the best time to achieve whatever goals you have.

Keep that in mind especially if you're afraid of change. In the next lesson, we'll talk about fear of change. Keep on reading!

CONFIDENCE AND GOALS
If you believe you *can't* achieve something, you're right. If you believe you *can* achieve something, you're also right.

See how that works? Confidence is that important to reach your goals. If you're confident, you won't stop at the first roadblock, because you know you can do it and you know that failure is not the end of your journey.

Think of a goal you have. Write it down. Maybe you want to start your own business? Maybe you want to reach a new audience? Maybe you want to get a promotion? Whatever it is, write it down.

Now write all the things, all the strategies you're willing to do to attain that goal.

Take a step back and answer this question: is your goal proportional to your strategies? If your goal is a big one, you'll need to work hard to attain it. I'm not saying you can't. I'm saying it's not going to happen over night.

Do you know why so many people don't stick to their new year's resolutions? They try to change their habit for a few weeks and then give up. But studies show that it takes 66 days to change a habit. Without self-confidence, you're not able stay on track. You don't see any change and you just give up. But with self-confidence, you know that the best is yet to come, you know that with patience and momentum, you'll eventually reach your goal.

If you want to learn more about this subject, I recommend the book *The Magic Of Thinking Big* by David J. Schwartz.

CONFIDENCE AND RELATIONSHIPS

See confidence as being your currency. You project a certain value of yourself to others. Even if they're not able to read your mind, they can analyze what you're saying, how you're saying it and your body language.

Remember that having self-confidence means you trust and respect yourself. When you are with friends, relatives, colleagues or clients, you project an image of yourself. The more self-confidence you have, the more people will respect you. They'll see that you trust yourself and they'll do the same.

Let's take a look at an example. One of my clients was struggling with her credibility as a communication strategist. She had several years of experience and had just started her own business. She told me that she had a hard time convincing potential clients to do business with her. Then I asked her: tell me why I should do business with you and not with someone else? All the answers she gave were okay but they didn't really answer my question. She told me that it's important to have a communication strategy, that an online presence is essential, and so on. But she didn't say a single thing about herself, her expertise or what makes her special.

Remember: People do business with people. This applies not only to entrepreneurs, but also to everyone who has to work or deal with other people: colleagues, clients, patients, relatives, friends, etc.

Basically, the only thing she needed to change in her pitch was to add her special touch, something that makes her services unique, because no one else can be just like her! But to do that, you need to trust and respect yourself.

Bottom line: self-confidence is an essential ingredient for healthy and respectful relationships.

CONFIDENCE AFFECTS YOUR HAPPINESS

Have you read the book The Secret? So many people were raving about it so I just had to get a copy. I'm sorry to say that I don't agree with it. I'm convinced that it's not the universe that holds the key to happiness. I know for a fact that you are the one who can change your life and your thinking. And I'm not the only one with this opinion.

Studies explain the real secret of The Secret. It's called RAS and it's all about your brain, your subconscious.

Have you ever noticed that when you're in the market for something, suddenly you'll see that something everywhere you go? Let's say you want to by a new car and your favorite color for a car is red. Every time a red car passes by, you'll notice it, right? Well that's because your subconscious is putting a lot of focus on red cars. It's like an information filter.

So you should add a confidence filter to your brain: a filter that blocks negative thoughts and welcomes positive ones.

When you're confident, you control your thoughts and therefore your life. And that's a big deal because happiness comes from your thinking. They're linked together.

Start listening to your thoughts. Are they contributing to your happiness?

CHALLENGES

Okay! It's time for your challenges.

Here are your challenges for today's lesson:

1. What do you do when you are faced with a challenge?
2. Why do you want to improve your self-confidence? What's your goal?

BONUS: Help other people boost their self-confidence. You can join our Facebook group to do so: Self-Confidence Boosters

LESSON 3
HOW TO BECOME A FEAR DESTROYER

To boost your confidence, you need to know what limits it. 9 times out of 10, fear is to blame. When we know where fear really comes from, we can start to control it.

So, now we know that confidence is a skill, that you need to train, and that confidence can change your life significantly since it affects all aspects of your life.

Today's lesson is the masterpiece of this book and also an important part of my programs.

Without further ado, let's begin today's lesson.

WHAT IS FEAR?
The simplest way to overcome an issue or a problem is to understand what it is. So let's take a look at what fear is.

Fear is an emotion of discomfort triggered by the belief that someone or something is dangerous, likely to cause pain, or a threat. Fear is a vital mechanism that is essential for survival. Without it, we would not be able to protect ourselves from a harmful situation.

That being said fear can also be counterproductive. We often fear situations that are far from life-or-death. The emotion may be real, but the cause isn't.

Recognizing that you fear certain situations is the first step toward destroying your fears.

What are you driven by? Fear? If that's the case, you're always walking on eggshells, never sure what to do or what to avoid.

It's really important to work on your fears, whatever they may be, because fear releases fear chemicals, which control your brain, your body and damage them. A build-up of fears can also lead to anxiety and aging, not to mention low self-confidence.

THE 3 MOST COMMON FEARS

FEAR OF FAILURE

So many people are afraid of failing and because they're afraid, they don't even try to accomplish their goals and dreams. It's sad because when you allow fear to control your life, you cannot reach your full potential. It's as simple as that!

And what is failure by the way? Failure is a learning tool. It should be seen as research.

You need to rewire your brain and encrypt this: the day I give up on my dream is the day I fail. You should try, fail, try again, fail better. To achieve that, get over things faster. Learn from your mistakes but don't stick to them. Let them go.

FEAR OF IMPERFECTION

Nothing is perfect in the world. Not even movies, pictures, speeches. Everything could be improved. So don't be a perfectionist. You'll waste too much time and energy for nothing.

Everyone has flaws. Everyone. I'm not saying that you shouldn't work on improving yourself. I'm saying to change your focus. Focus on what you're good at, what makes you special.

Also don't chase perfection. You'll chase it forever! Change your mindset. Chase progress. Don't over analyze everything. Have you heard of analysis paralysis? In short, it means you're over-analyzing everything so you don't actually do anything. Do something, even if you might find a better way to do it later. Take action, seek progress today, not tomorrow.

I encourage you to watch a video made by Dove. It clearly demonstrates how harshly we see ourselves and the difference between our perceptions of ourselves and how other people see us. Simply search *Dove Real Beauty Sketches | You're more beautiful than you think* on YouTube.

FEAR OF CHANGE

When we don't know what's coming, it can be scary. But like I said in the previous lesson, life is full of unexpected experiences. Even if we try real hard, we still cannot predict the future. I don't want to sound defeatist but the only thing we know for sure is that we'll all die someday. That's a fact! But we have no idea if it's going to be in 3 months, 3 years or 30 years. We have no control, no certainty!

Here's a tip you can use when you're still on the fence about something. Think of the best that could happen. Then think of the worst that could happen. Lastly, determine if it's worth it or not. By thinking of both ways, you'll make an informed decision.

MY TOP 5 TIPS

KNOWLEDGE

We live in a great era. Knowledge is now easily accessible on the Internet and, often, it's FREE!

Determine your fears and get some knowledge to help you destroy them. Your competence is your confidence and confidence is your competence. And how do we get competence? With knowledge.

FUNNEL YOUR PRIDE

Don't be too proud. It's okay to fail. Remember that failure is part of the learning process. To continue and learn from your mistakes, it's essential that you funnel your pride.

TRAINING

Practice is everything when trying to change a habit. If you tend to be controlled by your fears, train yourself not to react this way. Face your fears every single day, challenge yourself on a daily basis. The more you train, the easier it will become. Trust me!

FEED YOUR BRAIN WITH GOOD "BRAIN FOOD"

Like I said in the previous video, you should add a confidence filter to your brain, a filter that blocks negatives thoughts and welcomes positive ones. Learn to trick your inner voice. Let me tell you a great Native American Legend about feeding the brain with good "brain food".

> An old Cherokee is teaching his grandson about life. "A fight is going on inside me," he said to the boy.
>
> "It is a terrible fight and it is between two wolves. One is evil – he is anger, envy, sorrow, regret, greed, arrogance, self-pity, guilt, resentment, inferiority, lies, false pride, superiority, and ego." He continued, "The other is good – he is joy, peace, love, hope, serenity, humility, kindness, benevolence, empathy, generosity, truth, compassion, and faith. The same fight is going on inside you – and inside every other person, too."
>
> The grandson thought about it for a minute and then asked his grandfather, "Which wolf will win?"
>
> The old Cherokee simply replied, "The one you feed."

COURAGE

You have to have courage to do something even if you might fail, you have to learn to see fear and run towards it anyway. By facing your fears more often, you'll be able to build courage.

I want to share with you a quote that I absolutely love: "Courage doesn't mean you don't get afraid. Courage means you don't let fear stop you." This is a quote from Bethany Hamilton. She's an American pro surfer who survived a shark attack in 2003 and she lost her arm from this attack. Tragic and scary, right?

You know what she did after that? She got back up on her board and she went back out into the ocean. She faced her fears and because of it, she is still a pro surfer to this day. She is such an inspiration!

"Courage doesn't mean you don't get afraid. Courage means you don't let fear stop you." Remember that.

CHALLENGES

Okay! Time for your challenges.

1. [Watch Dove's video](): *Dove Real Beauty Sketches | You're more beautiful than you think*
2. Write down all the situations that trigger fear for you
3. Try each tip at least once during the upcoming week
4. Share with me how the training has helped you: marie@marieeveplamondon.com

To receive cool resources that will help you stay on track and reach your full potential, join the online family. Send me an email (marie@marieeveplamondon.com).

I'm sure you've learned a lot during this training and that's awesome. I'm glad you took action to change your life. But don't stop here! Use what you've learned on a daily basis and share your new knowledge with others.

And if you're really serious about boosting your self-confidence, check out my online programs. I'm sure I have one that's just right for you.

Okay, time to wrap up this book. Make sure to keep in touch with me for more motivational stuff.

Love,

Marie Eve
Your Self-Confidence Booster

ABOUT MARIE EVE PLAMONDON

Self-Confidence Booster. Fear Destroyer. Challenge Seeker. Chihuahua Lover.

Marie Eve Plamondon helps people reach their full potential and boost their self-confidence through online programs.

She's a self-made optimist and confident woman entrepreneur.

Printed in Poland
by Amazon Fulfillment
Poland Sp. z o.o., Wrocław